SAGGAR FIRING

IN AN ELECTRIC KILN

A Practical Handbook

Jolanda van de Grint

SCHIFFER PUBLISHING

4880 Lower Valley Road • Atglen, PA 19310

Copyright © 2021 by Jolanda van de Grint

Library of Congress Control Number: 2020952563

Some content was previously published in Dutch as *Saggar firing in een elektrische oven.*

Translation from Dutch: Jan-Pieter Schaper

Photography by Jolanda van de Grint
Designed by Yvonne van de Grint Grafische Vormgeving
Cover design concept by Yvonne van de Grint
Design production: Molly Shields
Type set in Sweet Sans Pro/Source Sans Variable

ISBN: 978-0-7643-6232-3
Printed in China
5 4 3 2

Published by Schiffer Publishing, Ltd.
4880 Lower Valley Road
Atglen, PA 19310
Phone: (610) 593-1777; Fax: (610) 593-2002
E-mail: Info@schifferbooks.com
Web: www.schifferbooks.com

MIX
Paper | Supporting responsible forestry
FSC® C104723

For our complete selection of fine books on this and related subjects, please visit our website at www.schifferbooks.com. You may also write for a free catalog.

Schiffer Publishing's titles are available at special discounts for bulk purchases for sales promotions or premiums. Special editions, including personalized covers, corporate imprints, and excerpts, can be created in large quantities for special needs. For more information, contact the publisher.

We are always looking for people to write books on new and related subjects. If you have an idea for a book, please contact us at proposals@schifferbooks.com.

Kiln manufacturers will void any warranty due to use of any combustible materials in their kilns. Saggar firing using combustible materials will decrease element life, as will every firing. It is not possible to determine how much each firing will shorten element life due to the amount of combustible material in the sagger, size of the kiln, duration of the firing, and number of firings.

Opposite: 2019
Sibelco 2502 with terra sigillata, diameter 15"/38 cm
Broken after bisque fire.

Page 4: 2018
Sibelco 2502 with terra sigillata, 9.4" x 7.8"/24 x 20 cm

CONTENTS

Introduction   7
What is saggar firing?   9
Trying to understand the process—my 2016 jars project   10
About this book   13
Environmental and health issues   15

1. **Making the saggar**   18

2. **Requirements your work must meet**   24
2.1 Clay type and surface of the work   25
2.2 Using terra sigillata   27
2.3 Bisque-firing temperatures   31
2.4 Glazing your work beforehand   33

3. **Materials that give color to your work**   36
3.1 Natural colorants   37
3.2 Metals   39
3.3 Oxides and carbonates   41

4. **Attaching the coloring materials to your work**   42
4.1 Natural colorants   44
4.2 Metals   45
4.3 Oxides and carbonates   47
     Results | before and after saggar firing   52

5. **Loading and firing the saggar**   56
5.1 Combustible materials   57
5.2 Loading the saggar   57
5.3 The amount of oxygen: Reduction and oxidation   61
5.4 Firing the saggar   63
5.5 Results and finishing   65

6. **Experimenting: Looking for new possibilities**   68
6.1 Experimenting with different types of saggars   71
6.2 Experimenting with clay and terra sigillata   73
6.3 Experimenting with combustible materials   75
6.4 Experimenting with coloring materials   75
6.5 Experimenting with firing methods   79
6.6 Experimenting with the finish   81

7. **When something goes wrong**   84

Work by workshop participants   86
Conclusion   91
Clays   92
Glossary   93
Acknowledgments   95
About the author   96

Instructions

Making a saggar   20
Recipe for terra sigillata   26
Applying terra sigillata   28
Attaching natural colorants to your work   44
Attaching metals to your work   45
Attaching oxides and carbonates to your work   48
Placing a single work in your saggar   58
Placing multiple pieces in your saggar   59
Reduction firing to get a black shard   76

INTRODUCTION

In 2006, I reentered the world of ceramics after 20 years. Not wanting to draw on my work from so many years ago, I started looking for new inspiration. In my photo collection I discovered a lot of pictures of old objects affected by time. These kinds of objects have always inspired me in my photography. Maybe I could let them trigger my imagination in ceramics too?

I particularly like the imperfection that results from an object's aging. Random patterns arise, which I find more interesting than contrived ones. The object looks lived through; it tells a story. My musings on this theme all fell into place when I found a book on wabi-sabi.* This Japanese aesthetic and philosophy dates back to the 15th century.

The core of wabi-sabi is to see beauty in "that which is imperfect, old, modest and authentic."

It is about appreciating the beauty in small things, and accepting that everything is transient and nothing is perfect. The use of natural materials and dark, modest colors is also part of wabi-sabi.

I wanted to capture this spontaneity and incorporate the unexpected results, beautiful details, dusky colors, and simplicity into my work.

In my search for suitable techniques I discovered alternative firing methods such as pit, barrel, and saggar firing, which appeared to be able to produce the colors, effects, and spontaneity that I was striving to achieve and which, for me, matched wabi-sabi. Pit firing and barrel firing produce a lot of smoke: those techniques are better practiced away from inhabited places. As I live right in the middle of town, these firing methods had to be discarded. For saggar firing, the book referred only to gas-fired kilns. Not having such a kiln at hand, I was left wondering if saggar firing could also be done in an electric kiln.

Wabi-Sabi for Artists, Designers, Poets & Philosophers by Leonard Koren.

Rotten wood and a wall with several old layers of paint   *A few layers of broken glass and a mountainside with signs of erosion*

WHAT IS SAGGAR FIRING?

The word "saggar" is probably derived from the word "safeguard." In wood-fired kilns, work that is being glazed is protected from flying ash by placing it in a separate, ceramic pot that is closed off before the firing. With saggar firing, you more or less do the same, but with the opposite purpose: the work to be fired is put in the ceramic pot together with certain combustible materials. The saggar becomes, as it were, a small wood-fired kiln inside your electric kiln.

In saggar firing, the end result is codetermined by materials that are put inside the saggar and fired together with the workpiece: combustibles, such as wood or hay, and coloring materials, such as iron oxide or copper carbonate. As we will see, best results are obtained by closely attaching these materials to the work. Choosing the right combustibles and coloring materials, you can influence the process and the end result—yet you will never be completely in control. The work that comes out of the saggar will be a surprise every single time.

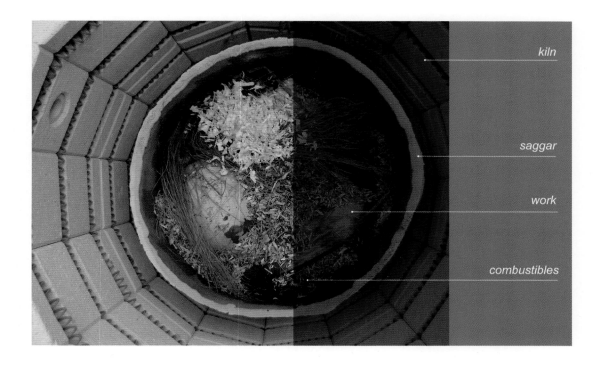

kiln

saggar

work

combustibles

JARS PROJECT 2016

Some jars from my project

You can find all jars on my website

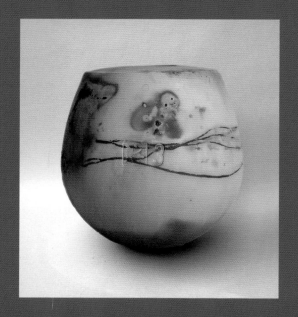  

There is precious little practical information about saggar firing to be found on the internet. There are descriptions of the technique and of the combustible and coloring materials that can be used, but exactly how to proceed is nowhere to be found. Moreover, opinions are divided as to whether saggar firing is at all possible in an electric kiln. In 2015, I decided to take the plunge and just get going.

In the beginning, results were very disappointing. An alarming amount of smoke emerged from my kiln during my first saggar firing, but my work came out without any color at all. With each firing, I kept adjusting things, using different combustible materials, adding greater or smaller amounts of oxides, allowing more or less oxygen into the saggar, and so on. Eventually, my pieces did gain some color, but still it was not at all clear to me how that had come about.

In order to get a good picture of the process and how different materials influence it, I clearly had to take a more systematic approach.

In 2016, I decided to saggar-fire one jar every week, for 52 weeks on end, as a test project. The jars were marked with my signature mark and the week number. I experimented with combustibles and coloring materials as well as with the firing process. This resulted in a series of 52 jars. I documented my way of working with photos and notes and I gained more and more insight into the effects of certain choices. At the end of that year I had learned a lot — and I had developed my own way of working.

I started to understand the process ever better, and more and more often my pieces acquired the colors and patterns I was looking for. Now do I fully understand how saggar firing works, and what exactly happens in the process? No, and I don't aspire to: I can influence things, but I'm not in complete control. For me, this unpredictability is precisely what keeps this technique so interesting.

Similarities in color and pattern between one of my jars (left) and an oil- and sand-stained wall (right)

ABOUT THIS BOOK

As results got better, I became more and more enthusiastic about this way of firing ceramic ware. People also responded positively to my results, and they shared their responses on social media. I started to regularly get questions about my working method. That's why in 2018 I decided to start giving workshops. Participants inspired me to do even more research and gather further information. This eventually led to the idea of writing this book and making the information I gathered accessible to everyone.

In this book I will show every single step, from making a saggar to finishing the pieces fired in it. I will describe what requirements your pieces will have to meet, which materials you can use, and which you'd better not. This book is the product of a personal quest. The method I describe will work, but undoubtedly it's not the only possible way of working. It does however provide a good basis to start experimenting for yourself. Every saggar, every kiln, and every firing will be different. That is exactly what makes saggar firing so appealing. I hope this book will provide you with plenty of tools to get you started on your own. Gradually you will gain more influence over the process, but you will not achieve full control; thus, every time you will be surprised by the result.

 On some pages you see this symbol. This is a tip or additional information.

IMPORTANT RULES

DON'T USE SULFATES, CHLORIDES, AND TABLE SALT (NaCL).
MAKE SURE ALL MATERIALS ARE COMPLETELY DRY.

ENVIRONMENTAL AND HEALTH ISSUES

Like many raw materials in ceramics, most oxides and carbonates are harmful for you and for the environment. The relevant safety information should normally be stated on the packaging. Make sure you take all the necessary safety precautions:

> Always wear gloves.
> Wear a tight-fitting mask over your nose and mouth.
> Do not work in an area where people also eat or drink.
> Keep oxides and carbonates out of wastewater as much as possible; for example, by using a sump or a sinking tank.

AT YOUR OWN RISK

Saggar firing in an electric kiln is safe, provided you follow a few rules. However, any firing you undertake following my descriptions is entirely at your own risk. I cannot be held liable in the event that damage occurs to your kiln. Or, for that matter, damage to anything else, or injury to any person.

IMPORTANT RULES

> Never use any table salt, sulfates, or chlorides in saggar firing! These will in time affect your kiln's heating elements.
> Make sure all materials you use are completely dry; any moisture will hinder the combustion process inside the saggar.

UTILITY WARE: NO-GO

Your pieces will come into direct contact with combustibles and coloring materials. For this reason, I would not use this technique for utility goods or functional pottery such as cups or plates.

 If you have a kiln that indicates its power consumption in kWh, it is useful to note, at each firing, up to what temperature (or cone number) you fired it and how many kWh that firing consumes. When you notice that firing starts to take more and more electric power, it is time to replace your heating elements. (All elements need replacement after a while, whether you do saggar firing or not. This is a way to monitor the condition of your elements.)

2020
Sibelco 2502 without terra sigillata, 9.8" by 9.8"/25 × 25 cm
Broken after bisque fire.

2019
Slip-casting clay with terra sigillata, 7.5" by 5"/20 x 13 cm

1. MAKING THE SAGGAR

It all starts with building the saggar. You will have to consider its size, its shape, and the type of clay to use. In the firing process, due to the combustion of the materials you are going to add, temperatures inside the saggar will rise faster than outside it. At cooldown, the kiln temperature will drop faster than the temperature in the saggar. The saggar must be able to withstand these thermal shocks. Furthermore, for fire to burn inside the saggar, oxygen must be able to enter. And at cooldown, some of the heat inside must be able to escape. Finding the ideal shape for a saggar is an ongoing process. Take a look at my website for my latest tips!

KEY CONSIDERATIONS
> Use a coarse grog clay, preferably raku or refractory (high-fire) clay.
> The best shape for a saggar is a cylinder, since that reduces the number of joins. Joins are vulnerable spots.
> Make all the saggar walls about 0.5"/1 cm thick.
> To ensure oxygen supply, make a hole of about 1"/2 cm in diameter in the wall, approximately 2.5"/7 cm below the top. In a saggar more than 10"/25 cm wide, pierce two holes, opposite each other.
> Take 11"/30 cm as a maximum for both diameter and height of the saggar. A saggar larger than that will become difficult to handle. In addition, the great amount of combustibles that such a saggar could contain would make it too hot, increasing the risk of cracking.
> Provide for a flat top side, so you can properly close off the saggar by covering it with a kiln shelf.
> Before using the saggar, fire it to a minimum of 2102°F/1150°C.

If you are good on the pottery wheel, you can also throw a saggar. Use a coarse grog clay.

WORKING METHOD
If the pieces of work you want to saggar-fire will always have the same shape, make your saggar just slightly larger than that shape, with a play of about 1.5"/4 cm all around and 2.5"/6 cm on top. Alternatively, you can make a saggar in which several pieces can be fired in a single batch.

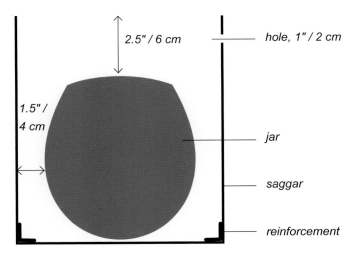

Figure 1: saggar for my jar project

Use a support shape that has the form and size you want your saggar to have: a large can, a big tube, or some similar object. Cover the support shape first with a layer of paper and then with a layer of plastic. This will make it easier to remove the support shape later on.

MAKING A SAGGAR | Instructions

1

Roll 0.5"/1 cm thick slabs for the saggar's bottom and wall. Cut the wall to the correct length and height. The ends must overlap on the support shape. Make these edges a little thinner than the rest of the slab. Allow the slabs to dry until they are more manageable but still bend well.

2

Place the support shape on the clay slab and roll the clay around the support shape.

3

Using a fork, score the overlapping edges and apply slip. Press the ends together tightly.

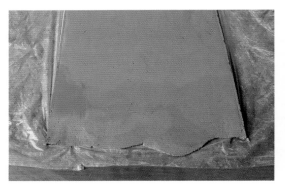

4

Set the shape upright and press the overlap just a bit more.

5

Find out where to place the cylinder shape on the bottom slab. Using a fork, score the bottom slab and apply slip.

6

Place the cylinder on the bottom slab and cut out the bottom, making it about 0.5"/1 cm larger than the cylinder.

7

Push the protruding edge upward against the cylinder with a wooden modeling tool. Then take out the support form.

8

Apply slip on the inside, at the join between bottom and wall.

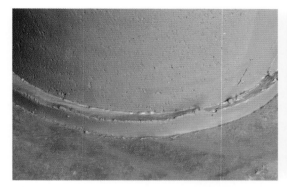

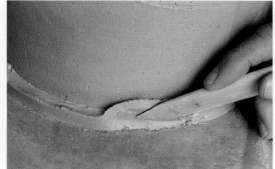

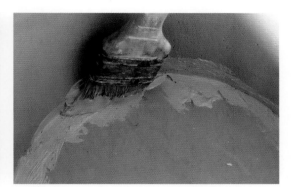

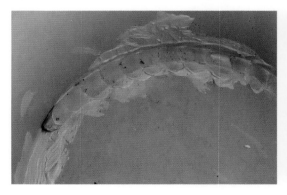

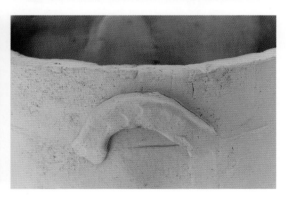

9

Apply a roll of clay to the join and press it, making sure no air is left underneath.

10

Cut a hole 1"/2 cm in diameter, about 2.5"/7 cm below the top of the wall. Make sure the top side is completely flat so that a kiln shelf can be placed on it.

11

With a larger saggar, it may be useful to add handles on the side wall.

2019
Slip casting with terra sigillata, 7.5" by 5"/20 x 13 cm
Fired in the saggar with copper wire, cobalt carbonate, and steel wool.

2019
Slip casting with terra sigillata, 4.5" by 10"/11 x 24 cm
Fired in the saggar with manganese dioxide, cobalt carbonate, and iron oxide.

2. REQUIREMENTS YOUR WORK MUST MEET

The size of the pieces you can fire is limited by the size of your saggar. As I explained in chapter 1, it is not wise to construct a saggar larger than 11" by 11"/30 x 30 cm. Large pieces are therefore not suitable for saggar firing. If you are looking for an alternative way of firing larger pieces of work, think of pit firing.

2.1 CLAY TYPE AND SURFACE OF THE WORK

You can use all types of clay for your work, both casting slip and molding clay, with or without grog. It is not necessary to use a special clay type, like raku. White-firing clay will give a white background, on which colors will stand out nicely. Colors will become even brighter when you apply terra sigillata to your piece (see section 2.2). Of course you can also use colored clay.

Saggar firing can produce quite busy-looking patterns and colors. These will stand out nicely on a smooth surface. I enjoy exploiting that. However, a rough surface can also yield very beautiful results.

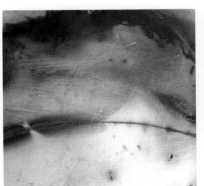

A smooth surface with terra sigillata   *A coarse surface without terra sigillata*

TERRA SIGILLATA RECIPE | Instructions

A very thin engobe for a slight sheen. Recipe with ball clay.

You could write a book in itself about making and using terra sigillata. I have one recipe that I use all the time, because it gives a nice, white terra sigillata.

RECIPE WITH 250-GRAM BALL CLAY:
> 0.55 lb. ball clay
> 0.84 pt. water
> 0.1 tablespoon sodium silicate
> 0.05 oz. sodium carbonate

If you want to make more or less, you can increase or decrease the quantities proportionally.

Add the sodium silicate and sodium carbonate to the water and make sure everything is dissolved.
Add the solution to the ball clay and stir well.
Leave this for at least 24 hours. You will see three layers: water (top, a very thin layer), terra sigillata (middle), and the more heavy particles (bottom).
The layer of water is so thin that I don't bother to separate it.

water

terra sigillata

heavier particles

Carefully pour the terra sigillata together with the water into a sealable container. The heavy particles remain on the bottom. The longer you leave it, the finer the terra sigillata will become. Stir well every time you use it.

Do not discard the rest of the ball clay.
Let it dry and use it to make an engobe or slip.

2.2. USING TERRA SIGILLATA

To give your work a light shine, you can polish it. But I always find polishing quite a chore. Another way to obtain a shine is to use terra sigillata. In addition to a shine, your work will also get a nice, white background and colors will become brighter.

Terra sigillata (literally: sealed earth) is a very thin, watery engobe that contains only the very lightest clay particles. Terra sigillata will lose its shine at firing temperatures above 2012°F/1100°C. If you are going to fire your work at such high temperatures, applying terra sigillata makes little sense.

You can buy terra sigillata ready-made or make it yourself. I make my own and I always use the same recipe, with ball clay, because this produces a beautiful, white terra sigillata. If you want a base of a different color, you can also use a colored terra sigillata.

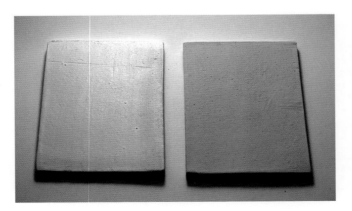

Sibelco 2502 after the bisque fire (1922°F/1050°C). Left with terra sigillata and right without terra sigillata.

APPLYING TERRA SIGILLATA | Instructions

Apply the terra sigillata to the bone-dry clay. This is best done using a slip trailer or other spraying applicator. You can also use a brush, but take care: you can easily wipe off a previous layer. When using a brush, apply three layers; using a slip trailer, two layers should suffice.

1 ─────────────
Place a drip tray (mixing bowl or the like) on a turntable.

2a ─────────────
Put a sieve inside the drip tray, in such a way that it does not stand on the bottom.

2b ─────────────
If your drip tray is larger than the sieve, put your sieve in upside down.

4 ─────────────
Place your piece in, or on, the sieve and spray on the terra sigillata while rotating.
Work quickly in order to minimize streaks. Cover the complete surface of your piece in one go. The terra sigillata runs through the sieve into the container below, thus preventing the piece from ending up standing in a whole layer of terra sigillata.

3 ─────────────
Fill one or more slip applicators with terra sigillata. The tip should be at least 2 mm.

If your work is too big for the sieve, place it on two slats above the drip tray. Use narrow slats and do not leave the work on it for too long, because you will soon see the imprint of the slats in the work.

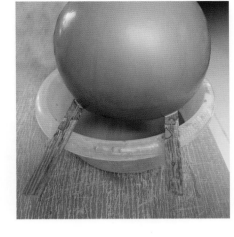

5 ————————————

Wait for the clay to absorb the terra sigillata. This occurs in only half a minute; the terra sigillata will then still be wet, but it will no longer shine. Spray on a second layer.

6 ————————————

The sieve remains wet, so once the terra sigillata has been absorbed, remove your work from the sieve. Once the piece has absorbed the terra sigillata, you can handle it without leaving fingerprints. Wait for a few seconds until the part that was in contact with the sieve has also absorbed all the terra sigillata, then put the work down. With pieces built from slabs, you will have to be careful that joints do not get too wet, which could make them come off again. Work quickly, and then blow-dry the piece. When the work is completely dry again, you can rub it with a soft cloth; this will make the shine even stronger.

Results of saggar firing at different temperatures of the bisque firing (casting clay)

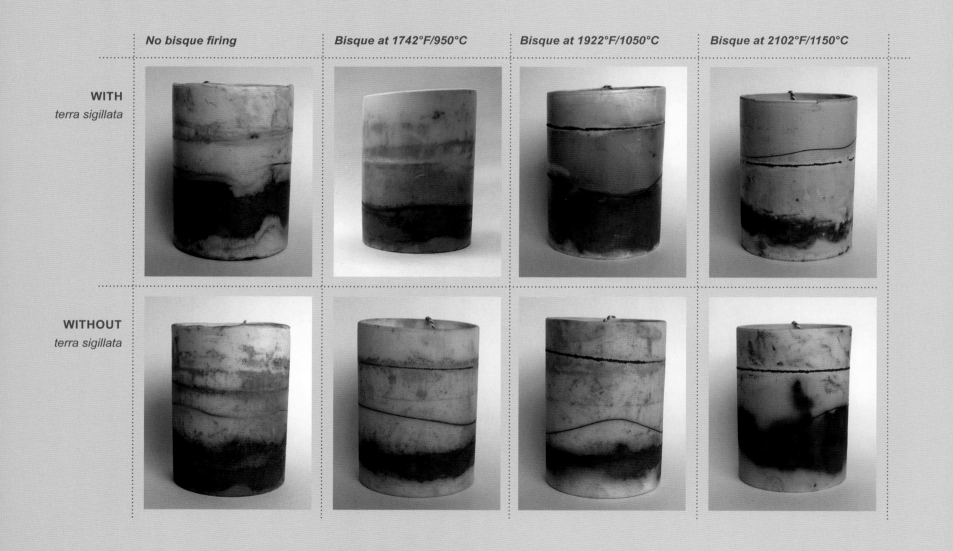

	No bisque firing	*Bisque at 1742°F/950°C*	*Bisque at 1922°F/1050°C*	*Bisque at 2102°F/1150°C*
WITH *terra sigillata*				
WITHOUT *terra sigillata*				

The pictures on the left show my results for a number of test cups. You will notice that the absorption of colors from added materials during saggar firing decreases sharply when the bisque firing is done at temperatures that exceed 1922°F/1050°C. There is little difference in color absorption between the test pieces that went without bisque firing and those that were bisque fired at 1742°F/950°C. However, the risk of breakage is much higher when saggar-firing unfired clay pieces. I therefore recommend to always have your work bisque fired first.

The images give a good indication of the results, but the outcome will not be the same for every type of clay. Moreover, in this series I used only copper wire, steel wool, and cobalt carbonate as coloring materials. Other colorants may give different results. So feel free to experiment with different types of clay and with other oxides and carbonates.

2.3. BISQUE-FIRING TEMPERATURES

I wanted to test the difference in color absorption during saggar firing for a range of bisque-firing temperatures. That is why I made test cups from casting slip, with and without terra sigillata. For good comparison of the results, I always used the same coloring materials: copper wire, steel wool, and cobalt carbonate. Amounts of steel wool or cobalt carbonate are difficult to keep exactly equal between tests. However, I was not interested in small variations due to a little more or less colorant; I wanted to see if any significant differences arose. All test cups have been fired at 1742°F/950°C in an identical-size saggar, with the same combustibles (wood shavings and hay) added in about equal quantities.

In the beginning I bisque-fired at 1742°F/950°C, because I assumed that colors would be less well absorbed by pieces fired at higher temperatures. After a number of tests I found that bisque-firing at 1922°F/1050°C also gives good results. The advantage of a higher firing temperature is that the piece will be stronger than when fired only up to 1742°F/950°C.

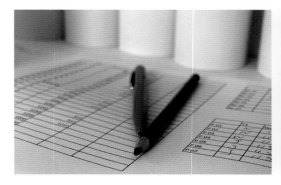

2.4. GLAZING YOUR WORK BEFOREHAND

With saggar firing, you add color to your work without using a glaze. Sometimes, however, you still want to glaze an object, such as a vase, on the inside. You can do so before or after the saggar firing. Glazing a work on the inside before saggar firing has a number of drawbacks: the glaze penetrates into the shard, which may reduce the absorption of colors during saggar firing. Ash particles can also get stuck in the glaze, and you will have to use a glaze that is fired at a maximum of 1922°F/1050°C. At higher temperatures, the shard will absorb fewer colors during the saggar firing (compare the results of different bisque-firing temperatures in section 2.3).

The best option is to glaze the inside after the saggar firing. The colors produced by oxides and carbonates will persist, and you can use any type of glaze, high or low temperature. Any blackness created by reduction (lack of oxygen in the saggar firing) will be fired out and disappear (more information on reduction in section 5.3).

Jar 29 was glazed on the inside before saggar-firing it. Because of that, the absorption of colors during the saggar firing is much less. The cobalt carbonate, which was attached to the work, is not even visible at all.

There are several products that you can use to waterproof your ceramics. However, none of these are permanent.

2017
Slip casting with terra sigillata, 5" by 4"/12 x 10 cm
In the saggar fired with steel wool, copper wire, and other pieces.

2017
Sibelco 2502 without terra sigillata, 9" by 4.5"/23 x 12 cm
In the saggar fired with steel wool, manganese dioxide, and copper wire.

3. MATERIALS THAT GIVE COLOR TO YOUR WORK

Only a small number of materials can give color to the work you fire in the saggar. This results in a limited but beautiful color palette. However, feel free to experiment with various materials. But do first check out carefully what each material is, because kitchen salt, other chlorides, and sulfates are out of the question: they will (eventually) damage your heating elements. Also avoid plastics. Any materials should be used only when dry.

Coloring materials for saggar firing can be divided into three groups:

> Natural coloring materials
> Metals
> Oxides and carbonates

3.1. NATURAL COLORANTS

Natural materials that can give color to your work are hard to find. Most natural dyes will burn at temperatures as high as those reached in saggar firing. Still, it is great fun to investigate the effects of the natural materials that you can find in your kitchen or garden. To really obtain some color on your piece, you usually will need a lot of the same material. You will need to both attach it to the work and put extra material in the saggar.

My research in this field up to now is by no means exhaustive, but I did try out a number of natural materials. Banana skins and seaweed gave me my best results.

Seaweed can give a nice red color.
Be careful: *seaweed contains salt, so use sparingly.*

Banana peels can give a pink color.

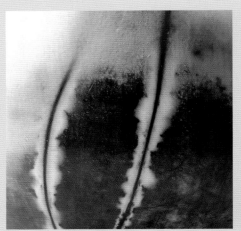
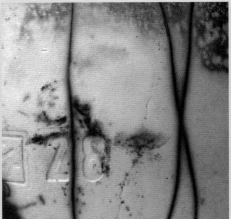
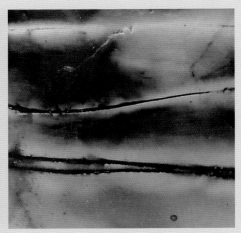

Three different results when using copper wire

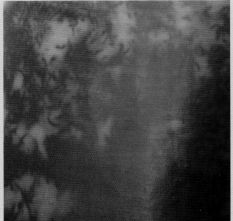
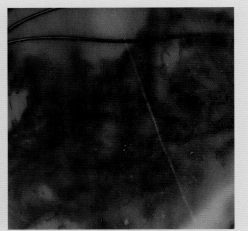

Three different results when using steel wool

3.2. METALS

Two metals that I often use as colorants, because they are easy to process and give nice results, are copper wire and steel wool.

Copper wire

For copper wire, a thickness of 0.4 mm will do. Using thicker wire is possible but will not give very different results. You'll find copper wire like this for sale at hobby stores, in the beads department. You can however also use the copper core from old power cords (thin twisted wires) or the solid core from electric wiring.

Copper wire basically gives black lines, but it can turn out differently under the influence of other simultaneously applied materials or a lack of oxygen.

Steel wool

This is a really rewarding material. It produces colors ranging from orange and pink to a very dark brown. You'll normally find it for sale in bulk-size packs at paint shops. Choose fineness grade 0000 (*four* zeros, that is).

The colors that steel wool produces on saggar fired work are very similar to those given by iron oxide, but steel wool is much easier to work with.

The coloring effect will depend on how far you pull the steel wool apart, on whether your work has been covered with terra sigillata, and on how closely the steel wool is fixed to the work during the saggar firing.

Oxides and carbonates

NAME	Red iron oxide	Copper carbonate	Manganese dioxide	Cobalt carbonate
MATERIAL				
POSSIBLE RESULT				
REMARKS	*The result will be somewhere between pink/orange and dark brown.*	*Gives basically black but will sometimes surprise you, since copper turns red in a reduction atmosphere (lack of oxygen)*	*A light- to dark-brown result (the dark line here is copper wire)*	*Different shades of blue*

3.3. Oxides and carbonates

Most of the coloring on saggar-fired pieces will have to come from oxides and carbonates. These are for sale at specialist ceramics shops. After I tried various oxides and carbonates, the ones that turned out to give the best results in the saggar were iron oxide, copper carbonate, manganese dioxide, and cobalt carbonate. The difference between oxides and carbonates is that oxides will generally produce a somewhat more intense color. Instead of copper oxide, however, I chose copper carbonate because it is easier to process. Iron oxide, which comes in different colors itself, always gives a result between orange or light brown and dark brown. I find red iron oxide hard to process, because the raw material is strong in color and difficult to clean up. Yellow iron oxide is easier to work with.

In addition to these oxides and carbonates, I have also tried chromium oxide, rutile, and stains. These three did nothing, colorwise, in a saggar firing at 1742°F/950°C. Chromium oxide is a dangerous, poisonous substance anyway, so you should avoid using it. Stains give little or no color to pieces fired in the saggar, and they are also relatively expensive.

Color intensity may vary from one firing to the next. It depends, among other things, on the type of clay used, on whether or not terra sigillata has been applied, and on the location of a piece inside the saggar.

On the left page you can see some of my results. The works were made of casting clay or Sibelco 2502 and covered with terra sigillata. They were bisque-fired at 1922°F/1050°C, and saggar-fired at 1742°F/950°C.

2019
Slip casting with terra sigillata, 8.3" by 5.1"/21 × 13 cm
Broken after bisque fire.

You now have a saggar, and one or more pieces you want to fire in it, and you have chosen the coloring materials you are going to use. The next step is attaching those materials to your piece, preparing it for the saggar firing. As you know from my introduction, I was not very successful in getting any colors on my work initially. I therefore wanted to get the coloring materials closer to the piece I was going to fire. Copper wire and steel wool can easily be attached to a piece, but for oxides and carbonates this is more difficult. I could paint them on, but that would destroy the spontaneity of color patterns appearing. Eventually I came up with the idea of gluing them onto combustible materials, such as cotton cloth and coconut fiber, and attaching these to the piece to be fired. This way I needed much smaller quantities of the oxides and carbonates to get good results.

Do not choose your best piece of work for your first saggar firing. You will need to do a few firings before you will begin to get a grasp of the process and be able to influence it. To start with, therefore, use pieces that you can freely experiment on without fear of failure. Also, try not to work with too much of a preconceived plan: that would destroy the spontaneity of your process, and results would still be different from what you imagined. Of course you don't have to use all of the coloring materials that I describe.

You will regularly need to use painter's tape to secure coloring materials onto your work. Always use small pieces: sometimes the tape will leave impressions on your work after the saggar firing.

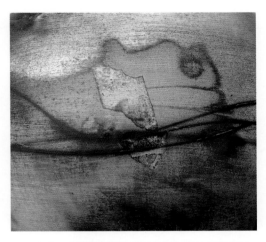

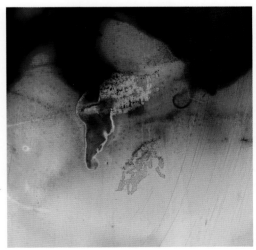

Impressions of tape used to attach copper wire (top) and steel wool (bottom) on a piece.

Natural colorants

4.1. NATURAL COLORANTS

For natural materials to work as colorants, you'll need a lot of them. Natural materials come in quite different shapes, so ways you can use to attach them to your work also vary. Coffee and tea could be fixed to the piece in the same way as oxides or carbonates: gluing them onto natural fibers. I use natural colorants fixed to my works to add an accent here and there, and sometimes I put them in the saggar separately—not attached to a piece to be fired—for a small additional touch.

Banana peels and seaweed can be fastened to your work with a thin cotton thread or sticky tape. You can pack your whole piece with them or concentrate them in just one place.

Banana peels attached to a work

Seaweed attached to a work

If you want to use natural materials, metals, and carbonates and oxides on the same piece, start with attaching the natural materials and metals to your work. They give the best result when attached close to your work, and you don't have to wear a mask and gloves yet.

Metals

4.2. METALS

Copper wire should always be closely attached to the piece you are going to fire.

Steel wool can also be put into the saggar separately; it will then give your work a pink glow.

COPPER WIRE

1 ——————————

Wrap copper wire tightly around your work. It must be snugly fixed onto the piece to get a good result. Tie it up by twisting the ends together, or secure it with small pieces of tape.

STEEL WOOL

1 ——————————

Lengthwise, tear off a piece of the steel wool.

2 ——————————

Do not cut off a small piece widthwise, because you will get only short, loose pieces.

3 ——————————

Carefully pull the steel fibers apart, as far as possible.

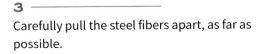

4 ——————————

Use cotton (or other natural) thread to tie the steel wool to your workpiece. You can have it cover a small part of your work or, like in this image, put it all over the piece.

4.3. OXIDES AND CARBONATES

As I wrote in the introduction to this chapter, I decided to glue oxides and carbonates onto a combustible support. In this way, the oxides and carbonates can be closely attached to the work. This requires some preparation, since there are a few extra things to consider.

When working with oxides and carbonates, use gloves and a protective mask!

GLUE

In the course of time I have been using different types of glue; mainly cheap, water-based adhesives. The point here is that your materials should not get too wet, but that the glue must be more or less easy to process (that is, it should allow for fast working). White household glue does not give a wet result, but brushing it onto the materials takes a lot of time. Gum arabic is also good, but quite expensive. I ended up with wallpaper paste as my go-to adhesive. It is cheap and works quickly, but it is quite wet, so you have to take that into account.

SUPPORT MATERIALS TO GLUE OXIDES AND CARBONATES ONTO

In principle you can use any natural substrate to glue oxides or carbonates onto. It is, however, helpful if the support material is flexible. I get my best results with materials that don't burn too quickly. When oxides and carbonates are glued to coconut fiber, the colors they leave on your work will generally become darker than when they are glued to a strip of cotton.

The materials I use most to glue oxides and carbonates onto:

Coir (coconut fiber)

For sale as nesting material at pet shops.

Thick rope

Make sure it is made of a natural material, such as hemp or jute.

Strips of cotton or linen

For example, from an old sheet. Here, too, make sure that it contains no artificial fibers. (See "At Your Own Risk" on page 15.)

Coconut fiber (coir)

Rope (natural material)

Cotton

Oxides and carbonates

SETTING UP

To be able to enjoy a smooth work flow, it's good to gather materials in advance.

Prepare wallpaper paste in a small, sealable 1-liter container or have some other glue at hand.

Put the oxides and carbonates in sealable containers of about 1 liter as well.

ALSO PREPARE THE FOLLOWING MATERIALS:

> Plastic place mats or some other pieces of sturdy plastic surface, preferably one for each oxide or carbonate
> Painters tape: stick a number pieces to the edge of your table
> (Old) newspapers
> Brush
> Very thin cotton (or other natural) thread
> A number of pieces of somewhat thicker rope and some strips of thin cotton cloth
> Gloves and mask

Manganese dioxide and red iron oxide quickly stain upon contact with water, and cobalt carbonate quickly becomes mushy. To ensure things don't get too messy and your work doesn't get covered in dirty fingerprints, it's wise to take a systematic approach.

If you have several pieces to which you want to attach oxides and carbonates, start out applying one single oxide or carbonate, attaching it to all the works. Return any remaining oxide or carbonate to its container. Clean everything, and only then start applying the next colorant.

Use the brush only for the glue; keep it free of any oxides and carbonates.

Do not let your materials and work(s) get too wet.

Wash your hands regularly so that you don't get stains on your work.

Make sure your hands are not wet with water or glue.

Using coconut fiber

1 ———————

Place a tuft of coconut fiber on an old newspaper or other scrap paper and, using a brush, apply a thin layer of wallpaper paste.

2 ———————

Place the coconut fiber on the place mat. Sprinkle it with an oxide or carbonate.

3 ———————

Let it rest for a moment, then tap off any loose oxide or carbonate.

4 ———————

Pull the coir slightly farther apart so as to get a larger surface.

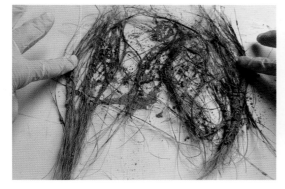

5 ———————

Fasten the coconut fiber to your work, using thread or tape. Return any remaining oxide or carbonate to its container.

6 ———————

With platters and bowls, the result will be more surprising when you put them in the saggar on their sides. To avoid any coloring materials falling off, you'll have to make sure they are firmly fixed to the piece(s) you are going to fire.

Oxides and carbonates

Using a strip of cotton cloth

1

Take a strip of cotton cloth and dip it into the wallpaper paste with a fork.

2

Then wipe the strip very well by passing it between your thumb and forefinger. You may really squeeze it; there certainly should be no more blobs of glue on it.

3

Then throw the strip in a container with oxide or carbonate in it, close the lid tightly, and shake a little. When you take the lid off, you will see that the strip is completely colored. Shake off any loose material before removing the strip of cotton from the container.

4

Place the strip on a place mat.

5

Put your work on the place mat, too, and tie the strip around it, fastening it with a knot, or attach it to the work using pieces of tape or cotton thread.

6

Return any remaining oxide or carbonate to its container.

Using hemp or jute rope

Hemp or jute rope can be used as a support for colorants in the same way as strips of cotton: dip it in the glue, then wipe it well. Put it in a container with an oxide or carbonate, put the lid on, and shake for a moment. Take the string out and shake off any loose oxide or carbonate.

You can then tie the rope around your work and knot the ends together, or secure the rope to the piece with thin cotton thread. Especially with smaller objects, the use of thin rope is useful.

When the oxides and carbonates are mixed on your place mat, you can put them in the saggar for some extra color or save them in a separate container for later use. Let the mix of colors surprise you.

PLATE

Steel wool

Coir with cobalt carbonate

Coir with manganese dioxide

VASE

Steel wool

Impression of tape

Copper wire

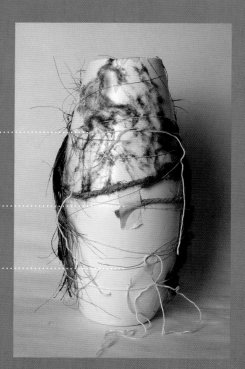
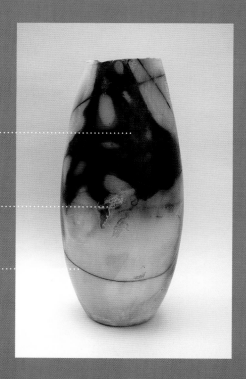

SPHERE

Coir with manganese dioxide ....

Rope with cobalt carbonate ....

VASE

Coir with cobalt carbonate ....

Rope with copper carbonate ....

Steel wool ....

2016
Sibelco 2502 with terra sigillata, 6" by 6.7"/15 x 17 cm

2019
Slip casting with terra sigillata, 6" by 6.7"/15 x 17 cm

5. LOADING AND FIRING THE SAGGAR

Now that coloring materials have been applied, you can install your work in the saggar, together with the combustible materials, and then put the saggar in the kiln. (See "At Your Own Risk" on page 15.) The results of your firing will depend on a combination of factors:

> The type and amount of combustibles in the saggar
> The position of your work inside the saggar (on the bottom or higher up; upright or on its side)
> The number of pieces you put into the saggar
> The amount of oxygen available in the saggar during the firing
> The firing temperature

5.1. COMBUSTIBLE MATERIALS

You can use various combustible materials for your saggar firing. These do not give color, but they do influence the color

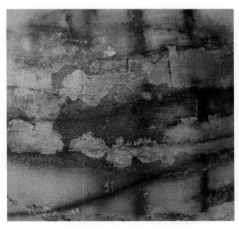

Dots created by adding pumpkin seeds

If you want to discover what the different coloring materials do, then use the same combustibles for each firing. For instance, use only hay and wood shavings.

patterns that will emerge. It is difficult to determine what exactly happens, but using, in the same firing, various combustibles that ignite at different moments does influence results.

In principle you can use any natural material as a combustible for your saggar firing. But anything you want to use should be dry before you put it into the saggar. Possible combustibles include:

> Wood shavings (available at pet stores for small pets). Do not use sawdust; this is much finer and more compact and therefore will not ignite as easily
> Hay (available at pet stores)
> Straw (available at pet stores)
> Paper
> Dry leaves, mosses, twigs, and other garden and floral waste
> Dried tree nuts
> Dried peelings of onions, potatoes, kiwis, oranges, avocados, and so on

I always use wood shavings and hay. When I strive to obtain some extra effect, I sometimes add other materials. You may also choose to use a single combustible material (see section 6.3).

5.2. LOADING THE SAGGAR

Wood shavings and hay that you buy in a shop will be packed tightly together in its packaging. Break or pull it apart to make it fluffier. Preferably do not use hay that has been cut into pieces shorter than 2"/5 cm.

You should also take into account the shape of your work. I put plates on their sides in the saggar. That way, the combustibles can move during the firing, which makes results more surprising than when the plates are installed horizontally.

Placing a single work in your saggar

1 ─────────

 Place a 0.5"/1 cm layer of wood shavings on the bottom of the saggar, and on top of that put a little hay.

2 ─────────

Place your work on these combustibles and then make sure to stack some hay along the sides of the piece. Do not push hard, to avoid overcompacting the combustibles.

3 ─────────

Also cover the top of your work with a thin layer of hay.

Placing multiple pieces in your saggar

Think about where in the saggar you want to put your pieces, and how (horizontally, vertically). Pieces placed in the lower part of the saggar often become a bit darker, because materials that fall from other works may fall onto them during the firing. The part of a work that faces the bottom of the saggar (the part sitting on the wood shavings and the hay) can turn black due to reduction (see next section).

1 ————————
Put a 0.5"/1 cm layer of wood shavings on the bottom and cover it thinly with some hay.

2 ————————
Place the first work (or works) on top of these combustibles (here: a plate sitting on its side).

3 ————————
Cover this piece with some more hay. Make sure there is always some hay between the pieces you put in the saggar together. You may safely stack multiple works.

4 ————————
Make sure there is also a bit of hay between your works and the saggar wall.

5 ————————
Continue until all the pieces you want to fire are installed in the saggar. Put some more hay on top.

Saggar firing does not need great quantities of combustible material. When you completely fill up the remaining space in the saggar with wood shavings, you'll get a lot of smoke—and very little result.

5.3. THE AMOUNT OF OXYGEN: REDUCTION AND OXIDATION

Reduction is a chemical process that arises from a lack of oxygen during the firing ("reduction firing"). It results in the shard of fired pieces turning black. The opposite of reduction firing is oxidation firing, which is firing with sufficient oxygen. A work that has turned black through reduction will regain its original shard color in a further oxidation firing. Reduction firing is possible only in kilns that allow regulating the amount of oxygen, such as wood- and gas-fired kilns. Electric kilns do not allow reduction firing.

With saggar firing, however, reduction can occur, because you fire in a separate container (saggar) with combustibles that need oxygen. You may influence the oxygen supply in that container (by making a hole in the saggar, or by stuffing that hole), but you will not have precise control over the amount of oxygen because it also depends on the combustibles you use: some combustibles use more oxygen. Moreover, during the firing you can no longer adjust anything at all. This makes it difficult to regulate reduction or oxidation. Your best chance for reduction is at the bottom of the saggar, where oxygen will be least available during the firing.

The black shard as a result from a reduction firing (top) completely disappears after an oxidation firing (bottom).

Copper turns red in reduction. In the photo you can see how a line made by copper wire has turned red.

Results at different temperatures of the saggar firing (casting clay)

| | Saggar firing 1562°F/850°C | Saggar firing 1742°F/950°C | Saggar firing 1922°F/1050°C |

WITH
terra sigillata

WITHOUT
terra sigillata

5.4. FIRING THE SAGGAR

Now your saggar is finally ready for the kiln. Cover the saggar with a kiln shelf. If there is no hole in your saggar (see chapter 1), make sure the shelf doesn't cover the saggar completely, so that it is not entirely closed off. Place the covered saggar on another kiln shelf. It is possible to fire several saggars at the same time in one kiln.

Temperatures for saggar firing

When I refer to the saggar-firing temperature, I mean the temperature set on the kiln's control unit. The temperature inside the saggar should normally attain higher values: that temperature will partly derive from the heat generated by your combustible materials. Although I usually do not fire my kiln up to more than 1742°F/950°C, in-saggar temperatures sometimes turn out to have risen as high as 1922°F/1050°C.

The test cups on the left show the results of saggar firing at different temperatures after a bisque firing at 1922°F/1050°C. Pieces saggar fired at 1562°F/850°C came out too pale, I found. In a saggar firing at 1922°F/1050°C, steel wool and copper wire may already start melting. Of course, here as elsewhere: feel free to experiment.

If you have the option, let the kiln cool down for a minimum of 5 hours, to 1022°F/550°C. The chance of your saggar cracking will be a lot smaller. The saggar, as it happens, cannot release its heat as quickly as the kiln itself. This may create a big difference between the temperature inside the saggar and that in the kiln, increasing the risk of your saggar cracking. Cooling down the kiln in a controlled way is all the more advisable for larger saggars (wider than 10"/25 cm).

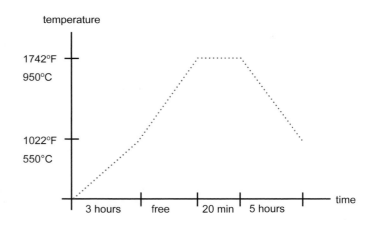

THE HEATING CURVE FOR A SAGGAR FIRING

I fire the saggar at 1742°F/950°C according to this heating curve:

> In 3 hours to 1022°F/550°C
> Then on to 1742°F/950°C in one go
> Hold for 20 minutes (i.e., keep at the same temperature)
> Let the kiln cool down to 1022°F/550°C in 5 hours

5.5. RESULTS AND FINISHING

It is advisable to let your kiln cool down to 212°F/100°C before opening it. Since temperatures inside the saggar will remain higher than those in the rest of the kiln for quite some time, the higher the kiln temperature when you open your kiln, the greater the chance that your saggar will crack.

The moment you open the saggar itself will always be exciting. One thing is for certain: the result will never be what you thought it would.

Using kiln gloves, remove the shelf that covers your saggar and take the saggar out of the kiln. You will see that not all the materials you added have been burnt up completely.

Take your work out of the saggar and clean the work thoroughly with water. Use a scouring pad if necessary. After drying, you can finally admire the result of your saggar firing.

If you are not completely satisfied, then that is a great opportunity to start experimenting. See section 6.6 for suggestions.

Finishing
Pieces that you are completely satisfied with may now be finished. I apply a turpentine-based furniture wax to works that I covered with terra sigillata before firing. I let the work absorb the wax for an hour, then rub it with a cloth. This will slightly enhance the delicate luster of the terra sigillata.

Glazing

Back in chapter 2, I mentioned glazing. If you want to glaze your work—for example, the inside of a vase—that can be your next step. What temperature the glaze requires is not important. Keep in mind that any blackness caused by reduction (see section 5.3) in the saggar firing will be fired out again and disappear in the glaze firing.

You can also apply a transparent glaze to the outside of your work. In that case, too, any reduction-induced blackness will disappear, but black coloring generated by copper wire or copper carbonate used in the saggar firing will turn green under a transparent glaze.

Copper usually turns green when you use a transparent glaze on top of the saggar-fired pieces.

2018
Sibelco 2502 with terra sigillata, 6" by 6.7"/15 x 17 cm
In the saggar fired with steel wool and copper wire.

2019
Sibelco 2502 with terra sigillata, 9.5" by 8.3"/24 x 21 cm
In the saggar fired with steel wool, cobalt carbonate, and iron oxide.

As you will have noticed in the previous chapters, many variables influence the results of saggar firing:

> The saggar itself
> The clay you use for your work and the finish you give it
> The coloring materials you apply
> The combustible materials you add
> The temperature and method you choose for bisque firing
> The finishing of your work after the saggar firing

You can vary any or all of these factors. In this book I have by no means described all the possibilities—I have not even tried all of them. That means there is ample space to experiment and discover new possibilities. This book is titled *Saggar Firing in an Electric Kiln*, so if you are going to experiment, do stick to the rules that apply to any firing in an electric kiln.

This means:
Do not use any salt, except for the carbonates mentioned in section 3.3. Specifically, do not use any sulfates or chlorides. Those may be used in pit firing, or in saggar firing inside a raku kiln, but not in the electric kiln.

Make sure all materials are dry.

Fill the saggar in an "airy" way. There must be enough air between the work or works and the combustible materials; otherwise you will get too little combustion, or none at all.

2019
Slip casting with terra sigillata, 8.3" by 5.1"/21 × 13 cm

6.1. EXPERIMENTING WITH DIFFERENT TYPES OF SAGGARS

For me, a ceramic saggar is ideal for use in an electric kiln. However, if you want to experiment with other types of saggars, there are several options.

Terra-cotta flower pots as a saggar

With some regularity, I am asked whether terra-cotta flower pots can be used as a saggar. I tried a few pots and got good results with pots with a thick wall (at least 0.5"/1 cm).

If you want to give it a try, take those 11"/30 cm as a maximum for the flower pot's top diameter. A larger pot will have to contain a lot of combustible materials and may therefore become too hot, so that the pot can crack, or even melt.

A saggar made of paper and clay slip

This saggar is built from layers of scrap newspaper coated with clay slip. You make this kind of saggar for single use, and for one single work. It is a lot of work, but it's fun to try. Unpacking such a saggar feels like opening a present.

A saggar made of aluminum

I have no experience with aluminum saggars myself. On the internet you will find various websites, mainly in English, describing how to work with aluminum saggars. This type of saggar is completely closed and therefore has less oxygen available for combustion. As a result, the outcomes will be different from those I describe and show in this book.

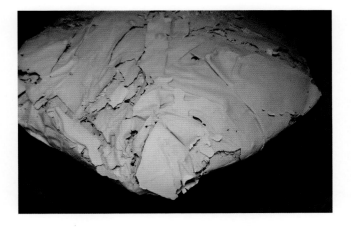

A saggar of paper and clay slip

Results of saggar firing at different temperatures of bisque firing (casting porcelain clay)

| No bisque fire | Bisque firing 1742°F/950°C | Bisque firing 1922°F/1050°C | Bisque firing 2102°F/1150°C |

6.2. EXPERIMENTING WITH CLAY AND TERRA SIGILLATA

Using other types of clay

In this book I mainly discussed work made of white-firing casting slip and fine or coarse grog clay. There are of course many more types of clay: porcelain, paper porcelain, and other white-firing clays. I encourage you to try out whether these give different results.

I made a number of test cups out of porcelain casting slip, without terra sigillata, because porcelain has a beautiful white color itself. The test cups were fired at various bisque temperatures and then fired in the saggar at 1742°F/950°C.

The results are shown on the left. The colors are brighter than with nonporcelain casting clay, but just as with those works (see section 2.3), the pieces bisque fired at higher temperatures clearly absorbed less color in the saggar firing.

Using clay in different colors

Nowadays there is a wide choice of colors for many types of clay. Just try some other clay color and see what result that gives. On an orange-firing clay, for example, a black color achieved by reduction firing or applying copper carbonate can be very attractive.

Creating variations with terra sigillata

In section 2.2 above, I discussed the use of terra sigillata. There, terra sigillata was applied to the entire piece. You can also choose to apply terra sigillata only to parts of your work. This gives you variations in both color and shine within a single work.

When applying terra sigillata to only part of your work with a slip applicator, you will generally get line patterns. If you want a more random result, you can coat your work with "wax-resist" in various places. Wax-resist is for sale at shops selling materials for potters and ceramists. You would normally use wax-resist before glazing, in order to prevent a glaze from adhering to certain parts of your work.

Allow the wax-resist to dry and then apply terra sigillata to your work. The terra sigillata will not adhere to the work wherever wax-resist has been applied. The wax-resist itself will burn off during the firing.

 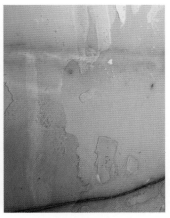

Test cup with partial terra sigillata. The colors and shine differ.

Results when using wood and/or hay during the saggar firing (casting clay)

Fired in the saggar:	Only a layer of wood shavings	Only hay under and around the piece	Both wood and hay
WITH *terra sigillata*			
WITHOUT *terra sigillata*			

6.3. EXPERIMENTING WITH COMBUSTIBLE MATERIALS

Firing with only one combustible material
The combustible materials you add play a role in the intensity of the colors your work will take and the patterns that will arise in the saggar firing. As stock combustibles, I use wood shavings and hay, but regularly I add some other materials.

You can experiment to see what happens when you use only one combustible material. Look for different flammable materials, such as orange peels, pine cones, acorns, moss, and so on. Also consider shavings from different types of wood, such as oak. Make sure they are dry, and always provide for enough space (= oxygen) between the combustible materials. Do not press your combustibles tightly together, and never completely fill the saggar with wood shavings (see section 5.2).

As examples, I fired these test cups in the saggar at 1742°F/950°C, with either wood or hay as the only combustible. The test cups were fitted with the same coloring materials: cobalt carbonate, copper wire, and steel wool. You can see the difference between the cups fired in the saggar with wood only, with hay only, and with both wood and hay. As you can see, hay has quite a big influence on the resulting colors.

6.4. EXPERIMENTING WITH COLORING MATERIALS
Start your own research into colorants by using natural materials from your kitchen, garden, park, or forest. You might get surprising results.

See what happens when you mix oxides and carbonates together before you apply them to your work.

After attaching the coloring materials to your work, additionally wrap it up completely in paper and then place it in the saggar. The coloring materials should stay in place a bit better.

Use different materials to make imprints on your work. You can use an oxide or carbonate to make imprints of certain materials; for example, feathers or leaves. Coat them with glue (just like the flocks of coir and strips of cloth in section 4.3) and sprinkle them with an oxide or carbonate. Shake off any excess material and attach the "oxidized" or "carbonated" feathers or leaves to your work.

REDUCTION FIRING TO GET A BLACK SHARD | Instructions

1 ————————

Place a 0.5"/1 cm layer of wood shavings on the bottom of the saggar and put a little hay on top of that.

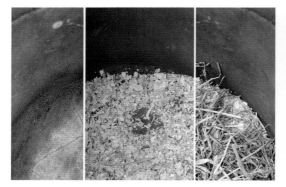

2 ————————

Put your work in the saggar and fill the saggar with combustible materials as usual.

3 ————————

Fill up the hole in your saggar with clay or a piece of kiln insulation blanket.

4 ————————

Cover the top of the saggar with a sheet of kiln insulation blanket.

5 ————————

On top of the blanket, you put a kiln shelf. Place the covered saggar in the kiln. The kiln needs to be fired only up to 752°F/400°C to get a good result.

6 ————————

Results: some shards of Sibelco 2502 with terra sigillata, fired in a completely closed saggar at 752°F/400°C

Using leftover materials from a previous firing

After firing, a bit of material will always remain in the saggar. You can of course completely clean these out before your next firing. You can also let yourself be surprised by leaving the remains in the saggar. The picture on this page illustrates that this will sometimes give remarkable results. The thin, white lines are from hay at the bottom of the saggar.

Blackening your work

Section 5.3 discussed reduction firing, which renders parts of your work black. In a saggar, reduction is difficult to control. However, you can choose to fire your work completely black. For that, you must ensure that as little oxygen as possible gets into the saggar. Note: in such a case, applying oxides or carbonates is useless, since they will give no visible result after the saggar firing.

6.5. EXPERIMENTING WITH FIRING METHODS

Firing the saggar at higher temperatures

In my current practice, I usually fire the saggar at 1742°F/950°C. But saggar firing at higher temperatures is definitely possible. You could fire up to the ideal temperature for the clay type you work with. For example, you could fire porcelain to 2102°F/1150°C or higher.

• ⋯⋯⋯⋯⋯⋯⋯⋯⋯⋯⋯⋯⋯⋯⋯⋯⋯⋯⋯⋯⋯

I have fired a saggar up to 1922°F/1050°C a few times. Copper wire and steel wool will then melt and get stuck on the work, creating a rough surface. If you don't want that, leave out these metals when you are going to fire at higher temperatures.

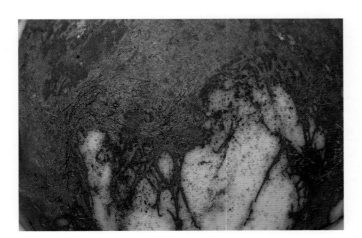

Firing in a raku kiln

A ceramic saggar is handy for use in an electric kiln, provided you follow the rules I describe in my introduction. If you have a raku kiln, it is also possible to fire the saggar in that. The advantage is that you can use other, additional coloring materials, such as salt and sulfates (but even when working outside, be careful with any vapors that come out of the barrel!).

It is important that sufficient oxygen can enter the saggar. The hole at the top of the barrel kiln must therefore remain open during firing. In that way, oxygen can get to the flame in the barrel but can also reach the saggar. You should prevent the flames in a raku kiln from directly touching the saggar.

The downside is that saggars often come out of a raku kiln cracked. You can try to prevent this by firing up slowly and cooling down in a controlled manner. If you really want to fire saggars in a raku kiln regularly, you will have to find out what the correct firing curve is. You can take the firing curve for an electric kiln (see section 5.4) as a starting point. If you use the coloring materials described in this book, results will not be very different from those obtained when firing the saggar in an electric kiln.

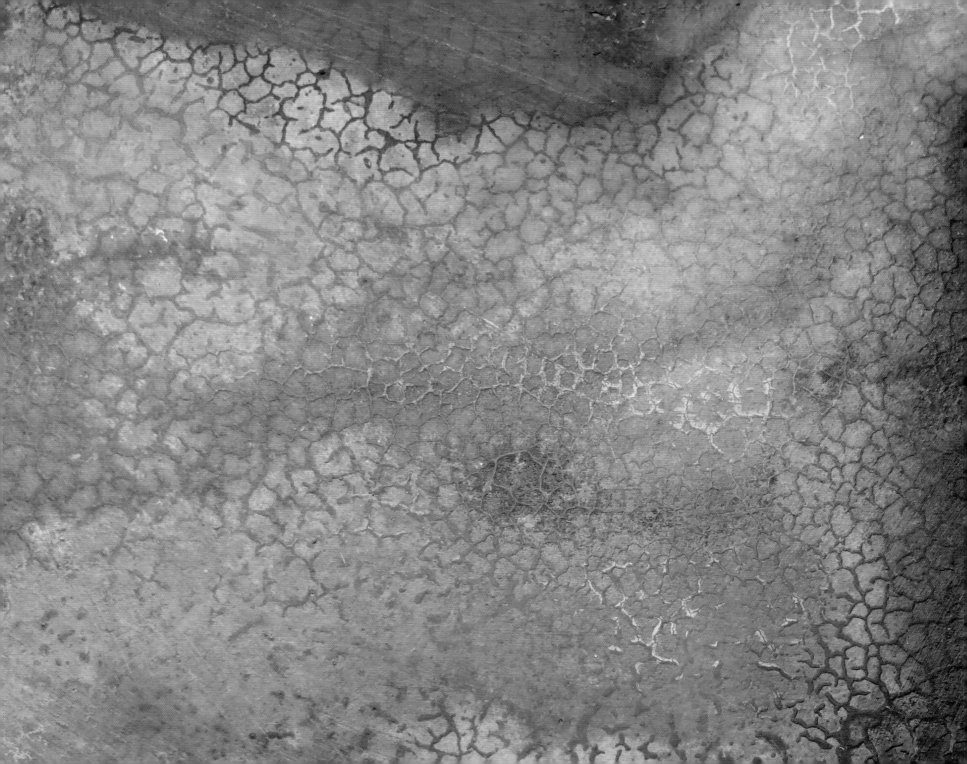

6.6. EXPERIMENTING WITH THE FINISH

Refiring pieces in the saggar

If you are not satisfied with your work or if you have a great appetite for experimenting, you can reattach some coloring material to your work and refire it in the saggar. Any black spots caused by reduction will disappear, though reduction may occur again in the new firing.

Applying terra sigillata after the saggar firing

Try to (re)apply terra sigillata to your work and include the piece in a bisque firing. This won't always work out well, especially when the work had already been treated with terra sigillata before the (first) saggar firing, but it can still yield nice results.

Refiring in the kiln at a clay's ideal temperature

In section 2.3 you could read that a high bisque-firing temperature reduces color absorption. If you used a type of clay that can be high-fired, such as porcelain, it is better to do the high-temperature firing *after* the saggar firing. You can then fire the kiln up to the ideal temperature for that clay type. Reduction blackness will disappear, but any other colors will mostly remain. I did this with two porcelain test cups. Both were bisque-fired at 1922°F/1050°C and saggar-fired at 1742°F/950°C. The one on the right was then again fired in the kiln at 2102°F/1150°C. The colors became beautifully bright.

Close-up of a work that's just out of the saggar and was wrapped in paper

Detail of a work with terra sigillata

7 WHEN SOMETHING GOES WRONG

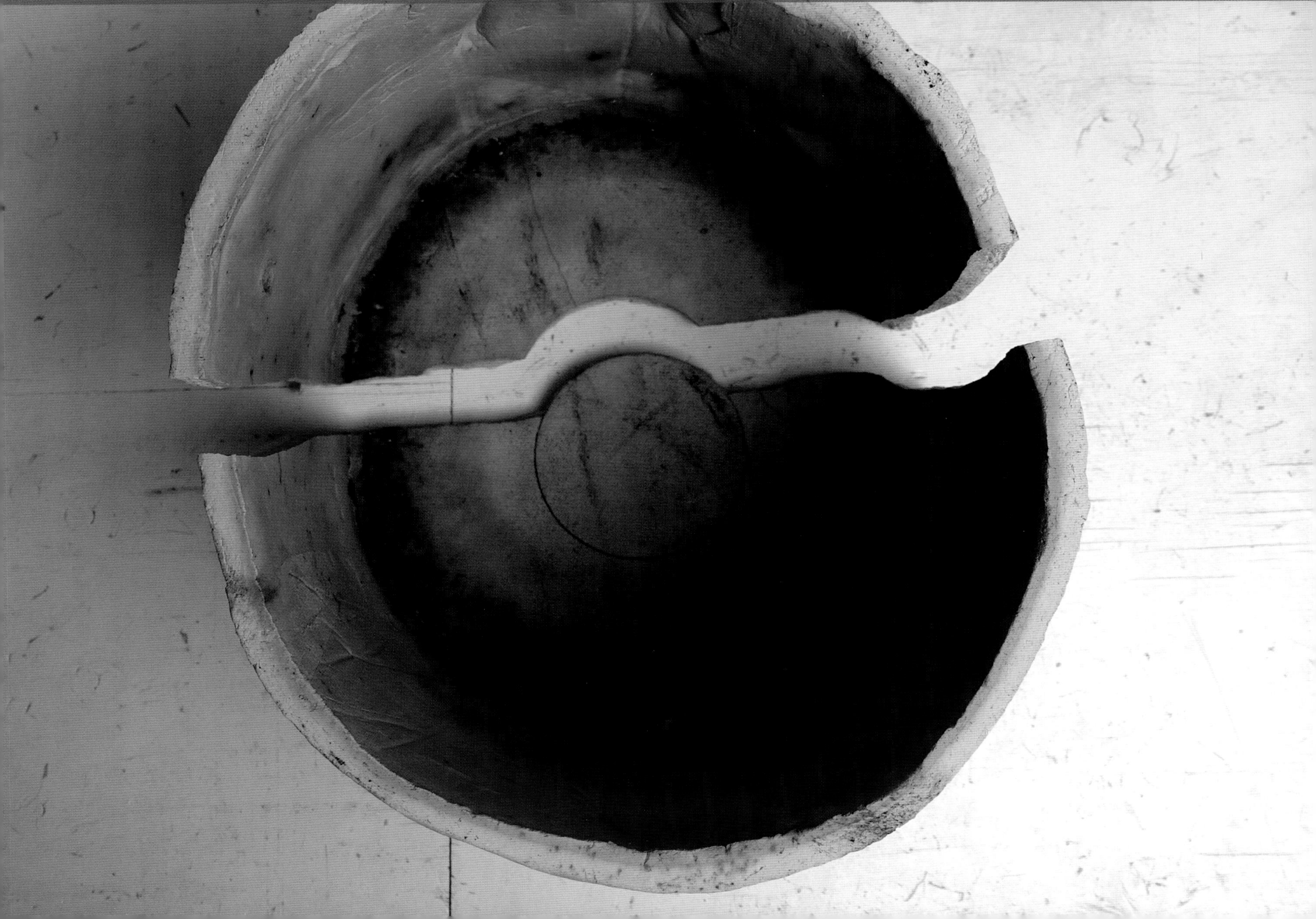

7. WHEN SOMETHING GOES WRONG

Despite all the good preparations, something can still go wrong. Fortunately, in some cases there is still something you can do.

Your work is too black
Cause: Most likely too-little oxygen came into the saggar during firing, probably because there is no hole in your saggar or because the hole was closed (see chapter 1).
Solution: Fire the work again on bisque temperature. If the black disappears, but no colors appear, you can attach coloring materials to the work and fire it again in the saggar. If the black has not disappeared, it is caused by an excess of copper carbonate or manganese dioxide.

The saggar is broken
Cause: Probably the temperature difference inside and outside the saggar was too large at some point.
Solution: Unfortunately there is no solution, but you can try to avoid it. See the directions for making a saggar (chapter 1) and the firing curve in section 5.4.

There's not enough color on your work
Cause: You have used not enough coloring materials.
Solution: attach coloring materials to the work and fire it again in the saggar (see chapter 4).

Cause: The coloring materials were not close enough to your work.
Solution: Attach coloring materials to the work and fire it again in the saggar (see chapter 4).

Cause: The work was fired too high beforehand (above 2102°F/1150°C).
Solution: Unfortunately, nothing can be done about this (see section 2.3 for bisque temperatures). Make sure that next time you don't fire above 1922°F/1050°C beforehand.

Terra sigillata has cracks or is peeling
Cause: The terra sigillata has been applied too thickly.
Solution: Next time, do not apply the terra sigillata too thickly. If you spray it with a slip trailer, don't do it more than twice. If you use a brush, apply a maximum of three layers (see section 2.2).

This is the work of people who have attended my workshops.
Photos from the participants' private collections.

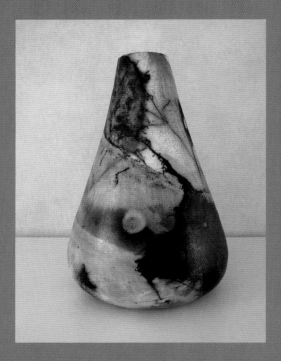

Jettie van der Zwet

Size: height 10.6"/27 cm, diameter (bottom) 7"/18 cm
Clay: White, grog: 25% (0–0.5 mm), max.
  temperature: 2336°F/1280°C
Terra sigillata: no, polished
Bisque temperature: 1742°F/950°C
Colorants: steel wool, copper wire, and a strip
  of cotton with cobalt carbonate, wrapped in a
  newspaper with leftover materials
Saggar firing temperature: 1922°F/1050°C

Karin Hoogendoorn

Size: height 9"/23 cm, diameter 5"/12.5 cm
Clay: White, grog: 40% (0–0.2 mm), max.
  temperature: 2372°F/1300°C
Terra sigillata: no, polished
Bisque temperature: 1832°F/1000°C
Colorants: cobalt oxide, steel wool, copper
  wire, dry leaves of a plane tree, dried manda-
  rin peels
Saggar firing temperature: 1868°F/1020°C

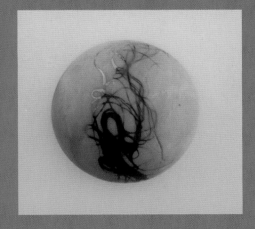

Krystyna Roeland

Size: height 8.5"/22 cm, diameter 4.5"/12 cm
Clay: White, no grog, max. temperature:
   2300°F/1260°C
Terra sigillata: yes
Bisque temperature: 1922°F/1050°C
Colorants: cobalt carbonate, copper wire,
   and inside small pieces of zinc
Saggar firing temperature: 1742°F/950°C

Juanita Delva

Size: height 7"/18 cm, diameter 5"/13 cm
Clay: White, no grog, max. temperature:
   2300°F/1260°C
Terra sigillata: yes
Bisque temperature: 1832°F/1000°C
Colorants: copper wire, 2 pieces of seaweed,
   manganese dioxide, steel wool, and cobalt
   carbonate
Saggar firing temperature: 1742°F/950°C

Netje van de Ven

Size: diameter 4"/10 cm
Clay: White, rest unknown
Terra sigillata: no
Bisque temperature: 1922°F/1050°C
Colorants: copper wire (from a power
   cord) and seaweed
Saggar firing temperature: 1742°F/950°C

Elly Walraven

Size: height 14"/36 cm, diameter 4.5"/12 cm
Clay: White, grog: 25% (0–0.5mm), max. tempera-
ture: 2336°F/1280°C
Terra sigillata: no
Bisque temperature: 1868°F/1020°C
Colorants: cobalt carbonate, iron oxide, copper wire
(0.6 mm), steel wool, and banana peel
Saggar firing temperature: 1742°F/950°C

Johan Ghesquiere

Size: height 8"/21 cm, diameter 7.5"/20 cm
Clay: White, grog: 10% (0–0.2mm), max.
temperature: 2336°F/1280°C
Terra sigillata: no, polished with sandpaper after
bisque fire
Bisque temperature: 1832°F/1000°C
Colorants: cobalt carbonate, iron oxide, steel wool,
palm tree leaves, and banana peel
Saggar firing temperature: 1742°F/950°C

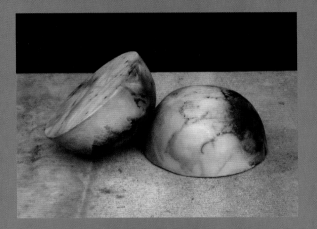

Frida Hengeveld

Size: height 4"/10 cm, width 7.5"/20 cm
Clay: White, grog: 25% (0–0.5mm), max. temperature:
2336°F/1280°C
Terra sigillata: no
Bisque temperature: 1805°F/985°C
Colorants: copper wire, flax rope with cobalt carbon-
ate Separate in the saggar: seaweed
Saggar firing temperature: 1805°F/985°C

Rita Hilhorst

Size: diameter 4.5"/11 cm
Clay: White, grog: 25% (0–0.5mm), max. temperature:
2336°F/1280°C
Terra sigillata: no
Bisque temperature: 1940°F/ 1060°C
Colorants: dried dung, cobalt carbonate, steel wool,
manganese dioxide, and small iron pieces in the
saggar
Saggar firing temperature: 1755°F/955°C

2018
Sibelco 2502 with terra sigillata, 9.5" by 8"/24 x 21 cm
Fired in the saggar with copper wire, manganese dioxide, and a little seaweed.

_____

CONCLUSION

At the beginning of this book, I promised to give you enough tools to get started with saggar firing in an electric kiln. I hope you feel ready to begin enjoying this method. Do not be discouraged when the first results are a bit disappointing. Document your process well with notes and photos, so that after a few fires you will get an idea of what is happening. In the long run you will be able to influence the result.

Are you on your own from now on? No, on my website you will find book titles and links to websites with even more useful information. I try to supplement it regularly. You can also join my Facebook group "workshop saggar firing." In that group you can see the work of others and ask questions of me and other members. This book contains the knowledge gained thus far in my work; I will continue to search for new possibilities. You can follow along on my website and via social media.

I wish you lots of ceramic pleasure, and I am curious to see your results.

2020
Slip casting with terra sigillata, 11" by 6"/28 x 15 cm

CLAYS

CLAYS
Used for making the saggar

Raku clay
> G&S 441 raku clay (45% 0.2–0.8 mm)
> Sibelco Raku 5015 (50% 0–1.5 mm)

Other clays used for work in the book
> Casting clay
> Sibelco HB 30 PM, white, temperature: 1868–2084°F/1020–1140°C
> Casting porcelain: temperature: 2102–2336°F/1150–1280°C
> Sibelco 2502: White, 25% grog size: 0.0–0.2 mm, temperature: 1832–2336°F/1000–1280°C
> Sibelco 2505: White, 25% grog size: 25% 0.0–0.5 mm, temperature: 1832–2336°F/1000–1280°C
> Sibelco 4020: White, 40% grog size: 40% 0.0–2.0 mm, temperature: 1832–2336°F/1000–1280°C

GLOSSARY

Ball clay
Plastic clay with a high shrinkage percentage. Is often mixed with other clays to make those clays more plastic.

Barrel firing
In a barrel firing, ceramics are fired in a barrel with wood and other flammable materials.

Insulation blanket
Special insulation material that is resistant to high temperatures. Made to isolate a raku barrel, for example. Available at most stores specializing in ceramic materials.

Pit firing
In pit firing, ceramics are fired in a large pit in the ground with wood and other flammable materials and coloring oxides and carbonates.

Raku
Raku is originally a Japanese technique. The work is given a special glaze. Then it is heated to about 1832°F/1000°C. At that temperature, the work is taken out of the gas oven and placed in a barrel with wood shavings. The wood catches fire immediately due to the heat of the work. Then the barrel can be closed for a while. The fire extracts the oxygen from the clay, making it black in places where there is no glaze. The glaze cracks, creating a play of black lines at work.

Reduction
The chemical process in which clay turns black due to a lack of oxygen during firing. This is possible only in a gas kiln or wood-fired kiln and to a limited extent in a saggar.

Slip trailer
A bellows in different sizes to apply slip and engobe to ceramics. A slip is a liquid mixture of clay. It's used to join parts of leather-hard clay. The slip is made of the same clay as the parts you want to join.

Terra sigillata
Terra sigillata (literally: sealed earth) is a very thin, watery engobe that contains only the very lightest clay particles. Applied to bone-dry clay, it gives the work a shine after firing.

Thermo-shock
A shock caused by a sudden, sharp change in temperature.

Wabi-sabi
Japanese aesthetics and philosophy dating back to the 15th century. The core of wabi-sabi is to see the beauty in "that which is imperfect, old, modest and authentic."

Wax-resist
A waxy material that is lubricated on bisque-fired work to prevent glaze from adhering there.

2018
Sibelco 2502 with terra sigillata, 10.6" by 4"/27 × 10 cm

ACKNOWLEDGMENTS

My gratitude goes to all the people who came to my workshops and with their questions stimulated me to keep experimenting. Also, to the people who gave me their permission to use their work in my book.

To Mirjam, Lilian, and Paula, for reading the Dutch version and giving constructive criticism.

To Yvonne, for the beautiful design. To Peter, for those crucial practical things, and to my family for their relentless support: Thanks! Also thanks to Jan Pieter for his translation and to all the people at Schiffer Publishing for their enthusiasm and hard work to get the English-language book out there.

Jolanda van de Grint found that the unpredictably beautiful aesthetic of alternative firing changed her art's focus. After years of research and experimentation with electric kiln capabilities, she now teaches workshops in saggar firing. She lives in the Netherlands.

www.jolandavandegrint.nl
www.facebook.com/keramiekjolandavandegrint
@keramiek_jolanda_vd_grint